The Mayflower Compact

by Jamie Kallio

Content Consultant
William Pencak, Professor of American History
Pennsylvania State University

CORE
LIBRARY

Published by ABDO Publishing Company, PO Box 398166, Minneapolis, MN 55439. Copyright © 2013 by Abdo Consulting Group, Inc. International copyrights reserved in all countries. No part of this book may be reproduced in any form without written permission from the publisher. The Core Library™ is a trademark and logo of ABDO Publishing Company.

Printed in the United States of America,
North Mankato, Minnesota
112012
012013
♻ THIS BOOK CONTAINS AT LEAST 10% RECYCLED MATERIALS.

Editor: Blythe Hurley
Series Designer: Becky Daum

Cataloging-in-Publication Data
Kallio, Jamie.
 The Mayflower Compact / Jamie Kallio.
   p. cm. -- (Foundations of our nation)
Includes bibliographical references and index.
ISBN 978-1-61783-711-1
1. Mayflower (Ship)--Juvenile literature. 2. Mayflower Compact--(1620)--Juvenile literature. I. Title.
974.4/02--dc22
                                        2012946531

Photo Credits: North Wind/North Wind Picture Archives, cover, 1, 7, 10, 18, 20, 24, 26, 33, 36, 39, 45; Peter Essick/Getty Images, 4; English School/Getty Images, 8; Betteman/Corbis/AP Images, 15; Steven Senne/AP Images, 28; Lisa Poole/AP Images, 35

Cover: The Pilgrims signed the Mayflower Compact in 1620 aboard the Mayflower.

CONTENTS

CHAPTER ONE

The Pilgrims

Imagine a continent filled with forests, rivers, and wild game. The land seems free for the taking. This is how explorers in the 1500s described America to the people of England. They hoped to convince other people to follow them to the New World.

European Expansion

The 1500s were a time of great growth for many European nations. Explorers traveled the world

The first English immigrants to the New World founded their colony in what is now Virginia.

claiming new land for their countries. New land was called a colony. Other people often already lived in these areas. But the colonists saw the land as theirs.

King James I believed England could profit from colonies in the New World. In 1606, the king gave a charter to the Virginia Company. This group planned and paid for new colonies. This charter was granted to settle the areas that are now Virginia, Maryland, and New Jersey.

In 1620, the Pilgrims set out for the New World with different goals. These men and women came to escape religious persecution.

The Separatists

During the 1600s, the Church of England was

Jamestown

Jamestown was the first English colony to survive in the New World. It was founded in 1607. The first decade was hard. During their second winter, food ran out. Out of 500 colonists, 440 died. This period was known as "The Starving Time." Jamestown survived and grew into a successful colony by the 1620s. It was an example for future colonists in the New World.

There is evidence the Jamestown colonists ate cats, dogs, horses, and rats during "The Starving Time."

King James I viewed religious groups other than the Church of England as troublemakers. They were often persecuted for their religious beliefs.

the official religion in England. Some groups wanted to separate from the church. They were known as Separatists.

King James saw the Separatists as troublemakers. They had no choice but to give up their religious practices, worship in secret, or leave the country illegally.

Emigration

After several arrests, a group of Separatists agreed to go to Holland. All Christians were free to worship there. In taking this step, they became pilgrims. A pilgrim is someone who travels to a foreign land because of their faith.

The Separatists landed in the city of Leiden, Holland, in 1608. Leiden was known for its cloth industry. The Separatists were mostly farmers. They had little skill in cloth-making. Because of this, they had to take the lowest-paying jobs.

The Separatists lived in Leiden for 12 years. Then they decided to journey 3,000 miles across the Atlantic Ocean to the New World.

Religious Persecution

King James I was head of the Church of England. Many religious groups asked him for changes to the church. He sponsored the creation of the King James Bible. This was a new translation of the text. But he refused to make other changes. He viewed other religious groups as a threat and passed harsh laws against them.

CHAPTER TWO

The Voyage

The Separatists believed they would have a better life in the New World. But they also knew there were risks. Beyond the dangers of the trip, there was the possibility of hunger and disease. There was also the risk of conflict with the Native Americans. Still, the Separatists continued to plan their journey.

The Pilgrims left Delft Haven, Netherlands, for the first leg of their long and difficult voyage to the New World. Women, children, and even animals were part of this punishing journey.

Slow Beginnings

The Separatists were not able to completely pay for their trip to the New World. They turned to a group of businessmen called the Merchant Adventurers.

At first, 125 Separatists planned to make the trip to America. But in the end, more than half decided to stay in Holland. The Merchant Adventurers added other people to make up the difference. The Separatists called them the Strangers. Together, this group would become known as the Pilgrims.

By the end of July 1620, the Merchant Adventurers hired a ship named the *Speedwell*. They also hired the *Mayflower*. Captain Christopher Jones and 30 sailors sailed the ship. Military officer Miles Standish joined to provide protection.

On July 22, the Pilgrims left Holland to meet the *Mayflower* in England. Then, on August 5, the Pilgrims set sail from Southampton, England.

A Troubled Journey

Trouble began right away. The *Speedwell* was leaky and unsafe. After several days of travel, the ships returned to England for repairs. A month of delays followed, and finally the passengers left the *Speedwell* behind. The *Mayflower* was loaded with 102 people and their supplies. On September 6, 1620, the Pilgrims were truly on their way.

The journey was expected to last two to three months. The Pilgrims feared their food would not last. Both Separatists and Strangers crowded into what was called the 'tween deck. This dark, cramped space was between the decks of

The *Mayflower's* Supplies

The Pilgrims didn't know when other supplies might arrive from Europe. So they brought many household items, including furniture and bedding. They brought weapons and armor as well as tools for planting and building. Livestock and pets were also brought.

the *Mayflower*. It was about 75 feet (23 m) long and not even five feet (1.5 m) high. All cooking, sleeping, and bathing were done in this small space.

The *Mayflower* met rough water and storms on the Atlantic Ocean. A violent wave broke one of the masts. Captain Jones almost turned around. But the Pilgrims lifted the broken beam into place so it could be fixed.

The weeks dragged on. Many of the Pilgrims began to show signs of scurvy. Two people grew sick and died.

After 65 days at sea, the New World was sighted on November 9.

The Compact

The *Mayflower* had landed on what would later be called Cape Cod. This was several hundred miles north of their planned destination. The group agreed to turn the ship around and head for their original destination, the Hudson River of the Virginia Colony. But within hours, the *Mayflower* entered Pollack Rip.

The Mayflower was estimated to be around 100 feet (30.5 m) long and 25 feet (7.5 m) wide.

This was an area of heavy waves and shallow water. The captain decided to turn back.

Some of the Strangers did not agree with this decision. By returning to Cape Cod, the Pilgrims would be breaking their patent, or agreement. The Strangers said once the *Mayflower* landed, they would leave the Separatists. This scared the Separatists. They felt the group needed to stick together to survive. Before anyone left the ship, the Pilgrims called a meeting in the *Mayflower's* main chamber. There, the Pilgrim leaders wrote an agreement.

In this agreement, the Pilgrims vowed to create a "body politic," or an organized group of citizens, to govern themselves. The agreement was a basic outline for how this government would work. It would have the power to make laws "for the general good of the colony."

On November 11, 41 men, both Separatists and Strangers, signed the agreement that became known as the Mayflower Compact. By signing this document, the men promised to follow their government and its laws. This was the first system of government created and carried out in the American colonies.

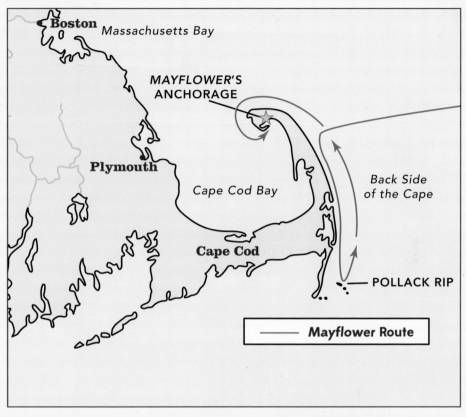

Boston
Massachusetts Bay

MAYFLOWER'S
ANCHORAGE

Plymouth

Cape Cod Bay

Back Side
of the Cape

Cape Cod

POLLACK RIP

—— **Mayflower Route**

The *Mayflower*'s Movements on the East Coast

The Pilgrims traveled thousands of miles across the Atlantic
Ocean to reach the New World, yet they did not land at
their intended destination, the Virginia Colony. Follow their
route from the back side of Cape Cod, down to Pollack Rip,
and back again to where they anchored at the wrist of the
cape in Provincetown Harbor. Compare the chart with the
description in this chapter. What might the Pilgrims have
done differently? What might have happened if they had
made it through Pollack Rip?

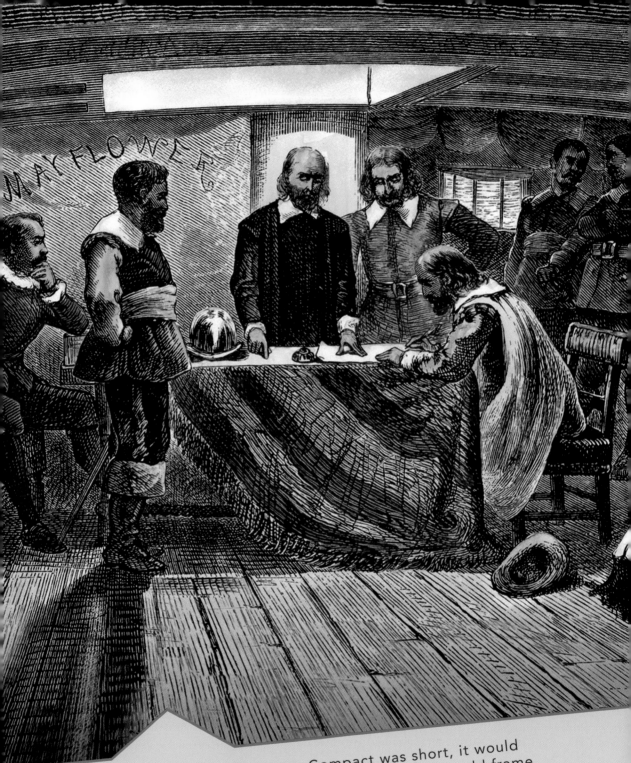

Although the Mayflower Compact was short, it would have an important influence on those who would frame the future government of the United States.

The Mayflower Compact

William Bradford's book *Of Plymouth Plantation, 1620-1647* has a record of the Mayflower Compact. It is outlined below.

> *Having undertaken . . . a Voyage to plant the First Colony . . . do by these presents solemnly and mutually in the presence of God and one of another, Covenant and Combine ourselves together into a Civil Body Politic . . . and by virtue hereof to enact, constitute and frame such just and equal Laws, Ordinances, Acts, Constitutions and Offices, from time to time, as . . . most . . . convenient for the general good of the Colony, unto which we promise all due submission and obedience. In witness . . . we have . . . subscribed our names at Cape Cod, the 11th of November . . . 1620.*
>
> Source: Bradford, William. Of Plymouth Plantation, 1620–1647. New York: Modern Library, 1967. Print. 75–76.

Think About Your Audience

Review the Mayflower Compact. How might you rewrite it for a different audience, such as your parents, principal, or younger friends? Write a blog post conveying this same information for your new audience. What is the best way to get your point across? How does your new approach differ from the original text, and why?

CHAPTER THREE

The First Winter

The Pilgrims had landed in early November 1620. They soon realized the area was too sandy and too close to the water. Miles Standish led a group of Pilgrims who went exploring. They searched for the right place to start their colony.

On their first outing, they met Native Americans from an unknown tribe. The Native Americans quickly ran away. During their second trip, they found Native

The Pilgrims made little progress in cutting lumber and building houses at Plymouth Colony before they became sick. More than half would not survive the winter.

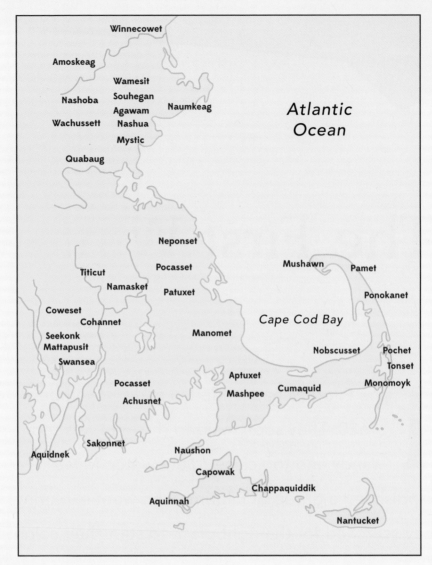

Winnecowet
Amoskeag
Wamesit
Nashoba Souhegan
Agawam Naumkeag
Wachussett Nashua
Mystic
Quabaug

Atlantic
Ocean

Neponset
Pocasset
Titicut Mushawn Pamet
Namasket Patuxet Ponokanet
Coweset
Cohannet Cape Cod Bay
Seekonk
Mattapusit Manomet
Swansea Nobscusset Pochet
Tonset
Pocasset Aptuxet Monomoyk
Achusnet Mashpee Cumaquid

Sakonnet Naushon
Aquidnek Capowak
Chappaquiddik
Aquinnah
Nantucket

Native American Place Names

Europeans felt the land in the New World was free for the taking. Yet as this map of Native American place names shows, local tribes had many communities in the area the colonists planned to settle. How do you think the Native Americans might have felt about the colonists' attitude toward their homeland? What can this map tell you about the Native Americans already living in colonial areas?

American burial sites with offerings of corn. The Pilgrims were worried about their own food supplies. They took as much corn as they could carry. They planned to repay the Native Americans someday, although it is not known if they ever did. In early December, the Native Americans and Pilgrims had a small fight. No one was hurt or killed. The colonists continued on. They hoped to explore the entire Cape Cod area.

In mid-December, the Pilgrims finally found the perfect spot. Captain John Smith, a member of the Jamestown Colony, had already explored the area and named it New Plymouth. It was

Common Diseases

The Native Americans had no protection against European diseases. In 1605, there were thousands of Native Americans living along the New England shores. But from 1616 to 1619, disease (possibly smallpox) wiped out much of the community. Many of the survivors fled. By the time the Pilgrims arrived in 1620, the Patuxet community had been left behind. The only signs that people had once lived there were piles of bones left throughout the area.

Great numbers of Native Americans died when they came into contact with European illnesses, against which they had no immunity.

protected by a large hill with a brook nearby. The area where the Pilgrims built their colony had once belonged to the Patuxet tribe. But it had been left behind after a great disease, leaving it empty when the Pilgrims arrived.

The Sickness

Poor weather kept the Pilgrims from building their colony right away. Snow was already on the ground when the Pilgrims started building on December 23. They planned to build a fort, 19 houses, and a common house for worship services and meetings. The common house was the first building completed. It was 20 square feet (6 m) and made of tree trunks and clay. It had a thatched roof.

The Pilgrims didn't get very far with building

The Little Ice Age

The Pilgrims soon found that summers were warmer and winters were much colder in New England than what they were used to. They had landed on Cape Cod during what is now known as "the little ice age," a period that lasted from about 1350 to 1850.

An ice age is a period of severe freezes during which glaciers cover much of the earth. But what the Pilgrims experienced during the little ice age was not one long freeze. Instead, they had to cope with violent swings in weather, including bitter winters, drought-ridden summers, and downpours in spring. These extremes lasted for decades.

The weather the Pilgrims faced in their first winter in the New World was bad. Extreme weather caused by a "little ice age" made life challenging.

before illness struck. In their weakened state, sickness spread among them quickly. The common house became a hospital. More and more of the Pilgrims fell ill. Finally, only seven were still healthy. Those seven nursed the sick and ran the entire colony that winter.

The death toll was horrible. By spring, the Pilgrims' numbers had been cut in half.

CHAPTER FOUR

The First Thanksgiving

The Pilgrims had met the local Native Americans a few times. They usually ran from the Pilgrims. So the Pilgrims were quite surprised when a Native American walked into their village on March 16, 1621. He was tall, with black hair that was short in front and long in back. His face was clean-shaven. He was naked except for a leather

A sculpture of Squanto can be seen at the Pilgrim Hall Museum in Plymouth, Massachusetts. He provided vital help to the Pilgrims.

fringe around his waist. Perhaps most surprising of all was that he called out, "Welcome, Englishmen!"

The man was named Samoset. He was a Native American chief. He was from Maine and had learned English from English fishermen. Samoset explained he knew a Patuxet man, Squanto, who spoke English even better than he did. Squanto could serve as interpreter to the local chief of the area.

Squanto, Lone Survivor

Squanto was originally from Patuxet. He was kidnapped by English commander John Hunt in 1614. Hunt sold Squanto in a Spanish slave market along with 19 other Indians. Squanto became a servant but escaped and traveled to London. Squanto returned to Patuxet in 1620 only to find that his people had been largely wiped out by sickness and his home had been left behind.

The Wampanoag

Soon the Pilgrims met Squanto. He set up a meeting with Massasoit, the chief of the Wampanoag people. They had been watching the Pilgrims all winter. A few days later, Massasoit arrived with 60 of his best warriors.

Edward Winslow welcomed Massasoit into the colony. Massasoit was very tall and his hair was greased back. He had painted his face and wore a necklace of seashells. Massasoit, Winslow, Governor John Carver, and William Bradford held a formal meeting to discuss peace terms. What the Pilgrims didn't know was that Massasoit was slowly losing power to a stronger tribe. Making peace with the Pilgrims was in his best interest, for it would give the Wampanoags an ally and trade partner. Massasoit and the colonists agreed to a treaty.

Massasoit's Treaty

The treaty between the Wampanoag and the Pilgrims did much to protect them all. Bradford recorded the treaty as such:

". . . they made a peace with [Massasoit] . . . in these terms:

1. That neither he nor any of his should injure or do hurt to any of their people.
2. That if any of his did hurt to any of theirs, he should send the offender, that they might punish him.
3. That if anything were taken away from any of theirs, he should cause it to be restored; and they should do the like to his.
4. If any did unjustly war against him, they would aid him; if any did war against them, he should aid them."

Spring Arrives

The Pilgrims were hopeful in the spring of 1621. The previous winter's illness had passed. They had good relations with the Wampanoag. And warm spring weather had finally arrived.

Squanto's help was very valuable. He showed the Pilgrims the best fishing places and helped them explore the area. He showed them how to use natural food sources, such as clams and eels. He taught the colonists how to plant corn, beans, and squash.

Without their Native American allies, the Plymouth colonists would probably not have survived to celebrate their first Thanksgiving. In fact, it is likely the Native Americans provided most of the food for their shared celebration.

Thanksgiving

The first Thanksgiving was not the same as the holiday celebrated today. But the Pilgrims had much to be thankful for. After such a hard winter, they finally had enough food.

After the harvest, Bradford declared they should all celebrate their good fortune. The Pilgrims and their Native American allies came together for three days of games and feasting. Most of the food for this celebration was probably provided by the Native Americans.

Many modern images of the first Thanksgiving are not accurate. The people did not sit at a long table covered in a white cloth. They probably ate standing up or used furniture from the Pilgrims' homes that was carried outside. Massasoit brought at least 100 members of his tribe to the celebration. They shared fresh-killed deer for the meal. They also probably ate wild fowl, dried corn porridge, and mashed pumpkin.

A statue of Chief Massasoit of the Wampanoag tribe can be visited in present-day Plymouth, Massachusetts.

CHAPTER FIVE

The End of the Mayflower Compact

Relations between the Native Americans and the colonists grew tense after the deaths of Massasoit and Bradford. Massasoit's son became the new leader of the Wampanoag. The colonists called him King Philip.

Philip did not trust the colonists. He felt they had broken the 1621 treaty by occupying land without his

On June 2, 1675, a group of Wampanoag attacked colonist settlements. The colonial militia fought back.

permission. They had also spread diseases among his people.

In December 1674, a Christian Native American colonist was murdered. Three Native Americans were put on trial and executed by colonists without Philip's consent. Among them was Philip's chief counselor. This set the stage for war. Fighting spread throughout the colony.

At first the colonists suffered greatly. Then, the colonists began to turn the war in their favor.

The war lasted 14 months. It was one of the bloodiest wars ever fought. Nearly 9,000 people were killed. The English made up one-third of the dead. Native Americans made up the other two-thirds. Out of the 90 towns in New England at the time, 52 were

While Plymouth Rock is a legendary location in American history, it is unlikely that the *Mayflower* actually landed there.

destroyed and left behind. Thousands of colonists became refugees. King Philip was killed.

The war greatly decreased the local Native American populations. Around 2,000 became refugees and left New England. Many who had been captured were enslaved. The Native Americans never regained the independence they had before the war.

The End of the Colony

The colonists had governed themselves based on the Mayflower Compact since 1621. But after King

Philip's War, the English government took a renewed interest in its colonies. Plymouth became part of the Massachusetts Bay Colony in 1691. The region no longer followed the Mayflower Compact. It would be decades before the colonies enjoyed self-rule again.

Legacy

The Pilgrims' way of life shaped early America. Many of their influences continue today. There is the tradition of Thanksgiving, a day of thanks in which the courage of the Pilgrims and the generosity of their Native American neighbors are remembered.

There is also the legacy of the Mayflower Compact. Its principles would be carried forward in both the Declaration of Independence and the Constitution of the United States.

Shots Fired and Blood Spilled

This record of King Philip's War from *A Brief History of the Warr with the Indians in New-England* includes the events leading up to the conflict.

One reason why the Indians murthered John Sausaman, was out of hatred against him for his Religion, . . . but the main ground why they murthered him seems to be, because he discovered . . . they were complotting against the English. Philip perceiving that the Court of Plimouth had condemned and executed one of his Counsellors . . . contrary to his promise . . . At the conclusion of [June 24th], . . . the Indians discharged a volly of shot . . . Thus did the War begin, this being the first english blood which was spilt by the Indians in an hostile way.

Source: Mather, Increase. A Brief History of the Warr with the Indians in New-England. 1676. Google Book Search. Web. 14 September 2012.

Changing Minds

This passage discusses the events that led up to King Philip's War. Who do you feel was to blame? Take a position, and imagine your best friend has the opposite opinion. Write a short essay trying to change your friend's mind. Make sure you state your opinion and your reasons for it. Include facts and details that support your argument.

IMPORTANT DATES

1606

King James I grants the first charter to colonize in the New World.

1607

Jamestown is founded in the New World.

1608

Separatists leave England for Holland.

1621

Half of the Pilgrims die during the winter.

1621

In March, Samoset arrives in the settlement; the Pilgrims meet Squanto and Massasoit. Massasoit, William Bradford, and Edward Winslow sign a treaty.

1621

The first Thanksgiving takes place to celebrate the first harvest.

1620

On September 6, the Pilgrims load everything onto the Mayflower and leave for the New World.

1620

Pilgrims see land on November 9. On November 11, the Mayflower Compact is written and signed.

1620

In December, the Pilgrims select a site for settlement, name it New Plymouth, and begin building.

1674

The Wampanoag attack and war breaks out in New England.

1676

The war ends, but the death toll is high. Wampanoag leader, Philip, is killed.

1691

Plymouth Colony officially becomes part of the Massachusetts Bay Colony.

Dig Deeper

What questions do you still have about the Pilgrims and the Mayflower Compact? Do you want to learn more about their everyday lives? Their interactions with local Native American tribes? Write down one or two questions that can guide you in doing research. With an adult's help, find a few reliable sources about this time period that can help answer your questions. Write a few sentences about how you did your research and what you learned from it.

Take a Stand

This book discusses the relationship between the Pilgrims and the Native Americans. Choose a position on the Pilgrims' treatment of the Native Americans. Write a short essay detailing your opinion, the reasons for your opinion, and some facts and details supporting your view.

Say What?

Studying the Mayflower Compact can mean learning new vocabulary. Find five words in this book you've never seen or heard before. Use a dictionary to find out what they mean. Then write the meaning in your own words, and use each word in a new sentence.

You Are There

Imagine you are one of the Pilgrims moving to the New World. Write 300 words describing your life. What were your experiences like during your voyage? What do you see when you arrive? What kinds of food do you eat? What do you know about the Native Americans living nearby?

GLOSSARY

charter
a written document that creates and defines a city, school, or company

compact
a formal agreement or contract between two or more people or groups

emigrate
to leave one's home or country to live elsewhere

patent
a document from the government granting the right to establish a colony on public lands

persecution
harassment of people who have a different religion, national origin, or system of beliefs

scurvy
a disease caused by a lack of vitamin C

treaty
an agreement between two or more parties about peace, trade, or other relations

LEARN MORE

Books

Fradin, Dennis Brindell. *The Mayflower Compact.* New York, NY: Benchmark, 2006.

Kallen, Stuart A. *Native American Chiefs and Warriors.* San Diego, CA: Lucent Books, 1999.

Yero, Judith Lloyd. *The Mayflower Compact.* Washington DC: National Geographic, 2006.

Web Links

To learn more about the Mayflower Compact, visit ABDO Publishing Company online at **www.abdopublishing.com**. Web sites about the Mayflower Compact are featured on our Book Links page. These links are routinely monitored and updated to provide the most current information available.

Visit **www.mycorelibrary.com** for free additional tools for teachers and students.

INDEX

ABOUT THE AUTHOR

Jamie Kallio is a writer and children's librarian living in the suburbs of Chicago. She has an MFA in writing for children and young adults from Hamline University and is the author of *Read On! Speculative Fiction for Teens.*